Do You Know Your

Bible?

A FUN QUIZ ON THE

Good Book

Wilson Casey

SOURCEBOOKS, INC.
NAPERVILLE, ILLINOIS

Published by Sourcebooks, Inc.
P.O. Box 4410, Naperville, Illinois 60567-4410
(630) 961-3900
Fax: (630) 961-2168
www.sourcebooks.com

ISBN-13: 978-1-4022-0884-3
ISBN-10: 1-4022-0884-7

Printed and bound in Canada
WC 10 9 8 7 6 5 4 3 2 1

1

Who is credited with being "Mother of All the Living"?

RUTH, SARAH, EVE, ESTHER

🌿

2

From Acts 18, who was Aquila's wife?

PRISCILLA, JEZEBEL, LEAH, REBEKAH

🌿

3

Where was Paul the Apostle born?

THESSALONICA, TARSUS, UR, ANTIOCH

🌿

4

Who was Timothy's mother?

ABIGAIL, MIRIAM, EUNICE, RACHEL

🌿

5

From Numbers 22, to whom did the donkey speak?

SILAS, DANIEL, JEREMIAH, BALAAM

🌿

6

From John 5, who stirred up the water at the Pool of Bethesda?

PRIEST, ANGEL, WIND, JESUS

🌿

7

Which city did Jesus not curse?

CHORAZIN, BETHSAIDA, CAPERNAUM, DAMASCUS

8

Who was Jacob's firstborn as found in Genesis 35?

REUBEN, EHUD, JOSHUA, ELAH

※

9

From Judges 1, who fed seventy kings at his table?

BENAIAH, NEBUCHADNEZZAR, ADONIBEZEK,
MEPHIBOSHETH

※

10

Which eighteen-year-old boy served as King of
Jerusalem for one hundred days?

SHAMGAR, JEHOIACHIN, ADINO, SISERA

※

11

To see Jesus, Zacchaeus climbed what type of tree?

FIG, CAROB, SYCAMORE, BOX

※

12

From Matthew 17, what did Peter find with a coin in
its mouth?

RAM, FISH, VIPER, RAVEN

※

13

Who were called "The Sons of Thunder"?

JAMES AND JOHN, THOMAS AND JUDAS,
PETER AND ANDREW, PHILIP AND MATTHEW

14
From Joshua 2, who hid two spies on a roof?
HOSEA, EZRA, SATAN, RAHAB

15
What was the first bird released from the Ark?
RAVEN, PIGEON, SPARROW, DOVE

16
From 2 Kings 9, what creatures ate the carcass of Jezebel?
SHE-BEARS, DOGS, FROGS, WORMS

17
Who worked seven years to earn a wife?
ISAIAH, ABRAHAM, JACOB, JOSHUA

18
From Joel 3, what was the mountain of the Lord?
SINAI, ZION, NEBO, MORIAH

19
On what day of creation was man created?
FIRST, SECOND, THIRD, SIXTH

20
How many windows were in Noah's Ark?
ZERO, ONE, FIFTY-TWO, ONE HUNDRED

21

From Proverbs 15, what does a soft answer turneth away?

WISDOM, SCORN, WRATH, FEAR

✤

22

Which Apostle was shipwrecked three different times?

PAUL, PETER, PHILIP, JAMES

✤

23

Who was David's father?

MOSES, NOAH, ABRAHAM, JESSE

✤

24

From Joshua 10, the sun stood still while Joshua's army destroyed what people?

AMORITES, MIDIANITES, EGYPTIANS, PHILISTINES

✤

25

Which apostle denied he knew Jesus?

JOHN, THOMAS, JUDAS, PETER

✤

26

From Genesis 9, who saw a rainbow in the sky?

ADAM, MOSES, NOAH, ABRAHAM

✤

27

Who was David's oldest brother?

JONAH, ELIAB, JOEL, AGRIPPA

28
From 1 Samuel 2, how many children did Hannah have?
FIVE, TEN, FIFTEEN, TWENTY

❧

29
After her first husband's death, whom did Ruth marry?
MALACHI, JOEL, CYRUS, BOAZ

❧

30
What name is shared by thirty-three people in the Bible?
DAVID, ZECHARIAH, DANIEL, HAGGAI

❧

31
Who fathered seventy sons with his many wives?
SOLOMON, JACOB, GIDEON, ESAU

❧

32
From Exodus 33, who saw the back of God?
ADAM, NOAH, ABRAHAM, MOSES

❧

33
Who had three hundred concubines?
PHARAOH, KING SOLOMON, SAUL, ADAM

❧

34
From Daniel 3, who saw four men walking in the
fiery furnace?
SOLOMON, JOB, DANIEL, NEBUCHADNEZZAR

35

With whom did Lot escape the city of Sodom?

WIFE, SON, TWO DAUGHTERS, TWO FRIENDS

&

36

From 2 Kings 9, who was thrown from a window and struck the ground dead?

HEZEKIAH, JEZEBEL, JOASH, ABNER

&

37

From Luke 1, what was Elisabeth and Zacharias's child named?

ELISABETH, ZACHARIAS, THOMAS, JOHN

&

38

From Genesis 4, who's considered the father of all musicians?

JEREMIAH, BOASH, JUBAL, JOB

&

39

From Luke 7, where did Jesus raise a widow's son from the dead?

AMOS, NAIN, LYSTRA, PHILIPPI

&

40

What Book's first chapter begins, "The former treatise have I made, O Theophilus"?

MATTHEW, LUKE, JOHN, ACTS

41

From Acts 9, where did Peter cure Aeneas?

TYRE, NEAPOLIS, LYDDA, GIBEON

❧

42

From Numbers 20, where did Aaron die?

MOUNT OF OLIVES, PISGAH, MOUNT HOR, GILBOA

❧

43

From 2 Kings 1, what Philistine city worshipped
Baal-zebub?

EKRON, SUCCOTH, GOMORRAH, ANTIPATRIS

❧

44

How many books of the Old Testament are divided
into two parts?

TWO, THREE, FOUR, FIVE

❧

45

How many books of the New Testament are divided
into two parts?

TWO, THREE, FOUR, FIVE

❧

46

Where do you find the phrase "God is love"?

GENESIS, NEHEMIAH, HEBREWS, 1 JOHN

47
What Jewish ruler visited Jesus by night?
HEZEKIAH, BARABBAS, NICODEMUS, DARIUS

※

48
How many suicides are recorded in the Bible?
ZERO, SEVEN, FOURTEEN, TWENTY-ONE

※

49
What Book's first chapter begins, "God, who at sundry times and in divers manners"?
MARK, GALATIANS, HEBREWS, JUDE

※

50
What were Gihon, Pison, Tigris, and Euphrates in connection with the Garden of Eden?
CITIES, KINGS, RIVERS, CAVES

※

51
From 1 Kings, who is given credit for writing 1005 songs?
JACOB, SOLOMON, PHILIP, DAVID

※

52
From Acts 13, where were Paul and Barnabas deserted by Mark?
JERICHO, PERGA, ATHENS, DAMASCUS

※

53
From Acts 5 and 12, how many times was Peter delivered from prison by an angel?
TWO, FIVE, A DOZEN, SEVENTY

54
Which Psalm is a Prayer of Moses, the man of God?
23, 90, 117, 150

❧

55
Who sold his birthright for a pottage of lentils?
CAIN, JACOB, ESAU, ABEL

❧

56
From Exodus 10, what was blown out of Egypt by a strong west wind?
RIVERS, LOCUSTS, SINNERS, NIGHTNESS

❧

57
From 1 Chronicles, who killed a seven and a half foot tall Egyptian giant?
BENAIAH, GIDEON, JANNES, BARUCH

❧

58
From Genesis 28, what city was the site of Jacob's famous dream?
LACHISH, PERGA, HARAN, BETHEL

❧

59
What Book's first chapter begins, "Paul, an apostle of Jesus Christ by the commandment of God"?
1 TIMOTHY, TITUS, JAMES, 2 JOHN

60

From Acts 16, what Asian city was the home of Lydia?

DERBE, THYATIRA, SAMARIA, JERICHO

※

61

From John 2, where did Jesus work his first miracle?

UR, CANA, ANTIOCH, THESSALONICA

※

62

From 2 Samuel, who killed a giant having twelve fingers and twelve toes?

MEPHIBOSHETH, JAMBRES, ABIMELECH, JONATHAN

※

63

From John 11, what city was home to Mary, Martha, and Lazarus?

CORINTH, GAZA, BETHANY, SARDIS

※

64

From Acts 10, what Roman soldier was led to Christ by Peter?

CORNELIUS, DAN, MENAHEM, FELIX

※

65

What was the aristocratic party of the Jews at the time of Jesus?

PHARISEES, REUBENITES, ISRAELITES, SADDUCEES

66

From 1 Kings 6, who built the first temple in Jerusalem?

SAMUEL, JOSHUA, SOLOMON, AARON

❧

67

Who was the wife of Moses?

NONE, ZIPPORAH, SUSANNA, RAHAB

❧

68

How many different foods are mentioned in the Bible?

NINE, TWENTY-NINE, FORTY-NINE, SIXTY-NINE

❧

69

From Genesis 29, which of Jacob's wives was first to bear children?

LEAH, RACHEL, BILHAH, ZILPAH

❧

70

From Acts 22, what famous rabbi was Paul's teacher?

HILLEL, TURKE, ZAKKAI, GAMALIEL

❧

71

Who stole idols from her father?

ELISABETH, MARTHA, RACHEL, DEBORAH

❧

72

From 2 Kings 16, who burned his son alive as a sacrifice?

JOAB, AHAZ, ISAAC, JOSIAH

73

From 2 Samuel 22, who said, "The Lord is my rock, and my fortress, and my deliverer"?

DAVID, SAMUEL, PETER, SOLOMON

74

2 Kings 19 and which other chapter are almost alike, word for word?

DEUTERONOMY 7, ISAIAH 37, JEREMIAH 50, JOB 16

75

"The book of the generation of Jesus Christ, the son of David, the son of Abraham" is the first verse of what Gospel?

MATTHEW, MARK, LUKE, JOHN

76

From Genesis 4, who invented farming?

ADAM, CAIN, ABEL, JUBAL

77

From Genesis 4, what righteous man started the practice of herding sheep?

ADAM, CAIN, ABEL, JOB

78

How many different people are mentioned in the King James Bible?

330, 930, 1,930, 2,930

79
According to Jesus, what was Satan from the beginning?
DECEIVER, EVIL, THIEF, MURDERER

80
In Biblical times, what was a large unit of money or weight?
LEVY, TALENT, SHEKEL, SEPULCHER

81
Who wasn't a son of Noah?
SHEM, HAM, LEVI, JAPHETH

82
From Matthew 13, what baking item did Jesus compare to the kingdom of Heaven?
EGGS, MILK, SALT, YEAST

83
Who tested the will of the Lord with a fleece?
JEHU, GIDEON, AMOS, AHAZIAH

84
From Micah 7:19, where does God place forgiven sins?
DEPTHS OF SEA, HEATHEN HEARTS, PAST THE STARS, FIERY PITS

85

Jesus said, "I am the Alpha and the _____"?

BETA, OMEGA, ETERNITY, DELTA

❧

86

From Psalms 60:8, David said, "Moab is my _____"?

TERRIER, WASHPOT, COURIER, WARRIOR

❧

87

What was the home of Peter, Andrew, and Philip?

CAESAREA, ASSOS, SARDIS, BETHSAIDA

❧

88

What type of water did Jesus offer the Samaritan woman at the well?

FRESH, COOL, LIVING, CLEAN

❧

89

Which was a type of food?

YOKE, MANNA, PRODIGAL, MINA

❧

90

From Matthew 9, after Jesus healed a paralyzed man, what did the man pick up and carry home?

BROTHER, BED, MOTHER, CART

91

Which Book begins, "And the Lord spake unto Moses in the wilderness of Sinai"?

EXODUS, LEVITICUS, NUMBERS, DEUTERONOMY

❧

92

From Exodus 7, what river was turned into blood?

RED, GALILEE, MARAH, NILE

❧

93

How many Books of the Bible have a name that is three letters long?

ZERO, ONE, TWO, THREE

❧

94

What prophet saw "the tents of Cushan in affliction"?

JAPHETH, NOAH, HEZEKIAH, HABAKKUK

❧

95

From Joel 2:6, what shall all faces gather?

SUNLIGHT, BLACKNESS, FEAR, WARMTH

❧

96

How many Books of the Bible begin with the letter E?

ZERO, TWO, FIVE, SIX

97
From 2 Timothy 1, who was Timothy's devout grandmother?
DORCAS, LYDIA, LOIS, HANNAH

⚜

98
From Judges 11, what judge of Israel was a prostitute's son?
HOSEA, JEPHTHAH, SAMSON, LOT

⚜

99
From Esther 1, what king did Esther marry?
JEHU, OMRI, AHASUERUS, ZEDEKIAH

⚜

100
Who asked, "If a man die, shall he live again?"
SAMUEL, JUDAS, JOB, STEPHEN

⚜

101
Which was a city of Ephraim and home of the Ark of the Covenant?
AI, SARDIS, GAZA, SHILOH

⚜

102
What Old Testament word means anointed?
BISHOP, MESSIAH, JEHOVAH, SALVATION

103

What prophet was the son of Elkanah and Hannah?

SAMUEL, HULDAH, DANIEL, NATHAN

104

From Song of Solomon 2, "The voice of the turtledove is heard in our land, for it is ____"?

WINTER, SPRING, SUMMER, FALL

105

How many times in the Bible do the words Christian or Christians appear?

ZERO, THREE, THIRTEEN, THIRTY

106

From 2 Samuel 4, what five-year-old boy was dropped by his nurse and made lame for life?

MOSES, MEPHIBOSHETH, PETER, ANDRONICUS

107

From Matthew 5, to what two things did Jesus compare believers, salt and ____?

WATER, BREAD, LIGHT, MOUNTAINS

108

Who became leader of the children of Israel after Moses's death?

ISAAC, JOSHUA, AARON, ABRAHAM

109

What was the trade of Paul?

SHEPHERD, CARPENTER, TENTMAKER, TAX COLLECTOR

110

From Genesis 31, who told Laban he had gone twenty years without a decent sleep?

ADAM, JACOB, MOSES, NOAH

111

Which book of the New Testament is divided into three parts?

CORINTHIANS, TIMOTHY, PETER, JOHN

112

From Numbers 22, what prophet had a talking donkey to ride on?

NIMROD, REHOBOAM, BALAAM, ZIMRI

113

From John 3, who asked, "How can a man be born if he is old?"

OBADIAH, NICODEMUS, JOSHUA, JOB

114

What was another name for the natural asphalt used to caulk Noah's Ark?

GOPHER, PITCH, CHIMERA, HELIOS

115

Which son of David was known for his good looks?

IBHAR, AMNON, NOGAH, ABSALOM

116

Who was the first person to go to heaven that didn't die in the flesh?

ELIJAH, MOSES, ADAM, ENOCH

117

From Acts 13, who was called "a man after thine own heart"?

DAVID, JOHN THE BAPTIST, GIDEON, PETER

118

Philippians 4:13 says, "I can do all things through ____"?

PRAYER, BELIEF, DEEDS, CHRIST

119

The Golden Rule is in chapter 7, verse 12 of which Gospel?

MATTHEW, MARK, LUKE, JOHN

120

From what were the clothes of John the Baptist made?

WHITE LINEN, SHEEPSKIN, SILK, CAMEL HAIR

121

From Numbers 14, of whom (in addition to Aaron) did God ask, "How long will this people provoke me?"

ADAM, MOSES, NOAH, DAVID

122

From Revelation 21, what perfectly square city is described as having walls made of jasper?

NEW DAMASCUS, JERICHO, NEW JERUSALEM, PHILADELPHIA

123

What was the home city of Joseph and Mary?

CAPERNAUM, NAZARETH, SHECHEM, BETHLEHEM

124

At the time of Jesus' birth, who was King of Judea?

SOLOMON, HEROD, BALAK, BELSHAZZAR

125

Gospel writer Luke said Jesus was about how old when he began to teach?

TWENTY, THIRTY, FORTY, FIFTY

Answers

1. Eve (Genesis 3:20)
2. Priscilla (Acts 18.2)
3. Tarsus (Acts 21:39)
4. Eunice (2 Timothy 1:5)
5. Balaam (Numbers 22:30)
6. Angel (John 5:4)
7. Damascus (Matthew 11:21–23)
8. Reuben (Genesis 35:23)
9. Adonibezek (Judges 1:7)
10. Jehoiachin (2 Kings 24:8)
11. Sycamore (Luke 19:4)
12. Fish (Matthew 17:27)
13. James and John (Mark 3:17)
14. Rahab (Joshua 2:1)
15. Raven (Genesis 8:7)
16. Dogs (2 Kings 9:10)
17. Jacob (Genesis 29:20)
18. Zion (Joel 3:17)
19. Sixth (Genesis 1:27–31)
20. One (Genesis 6:16)
21. Wrath (Proverbs 15:1)
22. Paul (2 Corinthians 10, 11:25)
23. Jesse (Ruth 4:22)
24. Amorites (Joshua 10:12)
25. Peter (John 18:25–27)
26. Noah (Genesis 9:13–17)
27. Eliab (1 Samuel 17:28)
28. Five (1 Samuel 2:21)
29. Boaz (Ruth 4:9–13)
30. Zechariah
31. Gideon (Judges 8:30)
32. Moses (Exodus 33:23)
33. King Solomon (1 Kings 11:3)
34. Nebuchadnezzar (Daniel 3:25)
35. Two Daughters (Genesis 19:15)
36. Jezebel (2 Kings 9:30–32)
37. John (Luke 1:13)
38. Jubal (Genesis 4:21)
39. Nain (Luke 7:11–12)
40. Acts (Acts 1:1)
41. Lydda (Acts 9:33–35)
42. Mount Hor (Numbers 20:26)
43. Ekron (2 Kings 1:3)
44. Three (1 and 2 Samuel; 1 and 2 Kings; 1 and 2 Chronicles)
45. Four (1 and 2 Corinthians; 1 and 2 Thessalonians; 1 and 2 Timothy; 1 and 2 Peter)
46. 1 John (1 John 4:16)
47. Nicodemus (John 3:2)
48. Seven
49. Hebrews (Hebrews 1:1)
50. Rivers (Genesis 2:11–14)
51. Solomon
52. Perga (Acts 13:13–14, 26)
53. Two
54. 90
55. Esau (Genesis 25:34)
56. Locusts (Exodus 10:19)
57. Benaiah (1 Chronicles 11:23–24)
58. Bethel (Genesis 28:16–19)
59. 1 Timothy (1 Timothy 1:1)
60. Thyatira (Acts 16:14)
61. Cana (John 2:11)
62. Jonathan (2 Samuel 21:20–21)
63. Bethany (John 11:1)

64. Cornelius (Acts 10:25–26)

65. Sadducees (Matthew 16:6)

66. Solomon (1 Kings 6:1–2)

67. Zipporah (Exodus 18:2)

68. Forty-nine

69. Leah (Genesis 29:32)

70. Gamaliel (Acts 22:3)

71. Rachel (Genesis 31:19)

72. Ahaz (2 Kings 16:3)

73. David (2 Samuel 22:1–2)

74. Isaiah 37

75. Matthew (Matthew 1:1)

76. Cain (Genesis 4:2)

77. Abel (Genesis 4:2)

78. 2,930

79. Murderer (John 8:44)

80. Talent

81. Levi (Genesis 6:10)

82. Yeast (Matthew 13:33)

83. Gideon (Judges 6:39)

84. Depths of sea

85. Omega (Revelation 22:13)

86. Washpot

87. Bethsaida (John 1:44)

88. Living

89. Manna (Exodus 16:15, 31)

90. Bed (Matthew 9:6–7)

91. Numbers (Numbers 1:1)

92. Nile (Exodus 7:20–21)

93. One (Job)

94. Habakkuk (Habakkuk 3:7)

95. Blackness

96. Six (Ecclesiastes, Ephesians, Esther, Exodus, Ezekiel, Ezra)

97. Lois (2 Timothy 1:5)

98. Jephthah (Judges 11:1)

99. Ahasuerus

100. Job (John 14:14)

101. Shiloh (1 Samuel 4:3–4)

102. Messiah

103. Samuel (1 Samuel 1:19–20)

104. Spring (Song of Solomon 2:11–14)

105. Three (Acts 11:26; Acts 26:28; 1 Peter 4:16)

106. Mephibosheth (2 Samuel 4:4)

107. Light (Matthew 5:13–14)

108. Joshua (Joshua 3:7–9)

109. Tentmaker (Acts 18:1–3)

110. Jacob (Genesis 31:39–41)

111. John (1 John, 2 John, and 3 John)

112. Balaam (Numbers 22:30)

113. Nicodemus (John 3:4)

114. Pitch (Genesis 6:14)

115. Absalom (2 Samuel 13:1, 14:25)

116. Enoch (Genesis 5:24)

117. David (Acts 13:22)

118. Christ

119. Matthew (Matthew 7:12)

120. Camel hair (Mark 1:6)

121. Moses (Numbers 14:26–27)

122. New Jerusalem (Revelation 21:16–18)

123. Nazareth (Luke 1:26–27)

124. Herod (Luke 1:5)

125. Thirty (Luke 3:23)

About the Author

W ilson Casey, aka The Trivia Guy, is one of the country's foremost trivia aficionados, with a syndicated column, an award-winning website (TriviaGuy.com), and a place in the *Guinness Book of World Records* for the longest-running (thirty hours) radio trivia broadcast. His weekly Bible Trivia column runs in over one hundred newspapers around the country and is syndicated by King Weekly Features.